For The Lost Boys

For the Lost Boys

JEFFREY FRANKLIN

GHOST ROAD PRESS

Library of Congress Cataloging-in-Publication Data.
Ghost Road Press
For the Lost Boys

ISBN 0977803481 (Trade Paperback)
Library of Congress Control Number: 2006932398

Book Design: Sonya Unrein
Cover painting: Jim Franklin
Author Photo: Andrew Clark

Ghost Road Press, Denver, Colorado
ghostroadpress.com

ACKNOWLEDGMENTS

Grateful acknowledgement is made to the following journals in which earlier versions of these poems appeared and to those editors whose decisions have supported my poetry:

Arts & Letters: "Drucker's Mule Barn"; *Asheville Poetry Review*: "Black Pattern on a Mocha Ground"; *Cider Press Review*: "Homosassa"; *Cimarron Review*: "Explaining to my Mother why the Next War will be Necessary"; *Crab Orchard Review*: "Cookin' with the David Jones Trio"; *Cutthroat*: "All the Connections" and "First Fall"; *Devil's Millhopper*: "Stories that Become Us"; *The Eleventh Muse*: "Dear Tooth Fairy,"; *Hiram Poetry Review*: "The Art of Building a Fire"; *Icarus*: "A Day's Outing"; *Isotope: A Journal of Literary Nature and Science Writing*: "Reasons for Lawns"; *Many Mountains Moving*: "Blind Jeff Death Revisits #3 Clark Road," "I Painted the House Myself," and "No. 9 Bluff View"; *North Carolina Literary Review*: "What the Rain Said this Morning"; *Now & Then*: "Tennessee Latitudes"; *Painted Bride Quarterly*: "Boundaries of Seeing"; *Poet Lore*: "'Blow, Wind! Come Wrack!'"; *Plainsongs*: "Breanna's Grandmother"; *Potomac Review*: "Facing the Elk"; *Quadrant (Australia)*: "Kakadu Cave Paintings"; *Southern Humanities Review*: "Days-o'-Work"; *Southern Poetry Review*: "Melos, the Usual"; *Square Lake*: "Slides of the Field Trip"; *Tar River Poetry*: "The Anthropology of Little League Baseball," "Elemental," and "In Jenny-Lynn's Garden"; *Third Coast*: "Judy as Piñata."

"Boundaries of Seeing," "Cookin' with the David Jones Trio," "Judy as Piñata," and "Kakadu Cave Paintings" (as part one of "Arnhem Land: Reading the Signs") were included in a manuscript that was co-recipient of the 2001 Robert H. Winner Memorial Award from The Poetry Society of America, for which I am grateful to the Society, to Stephanie Strickland, and especially to Sylvia Winner.

"Black Pattern on a Mocha Ground" was reprinted in *Best of Asheville Poetry Review 1994-2004*, thanks to Keith Flynn.

"Boundaries of Seeing" was reprinted in *Painted Bride Quarterly: Print Annual 1 (2003)*.

"At the Pilar Yacht Club," "The Mountain Lion at Bear Creek Archery" and "The Seeds of Sorrow" were anthologized in *Open Windows 2005* from Ghost Road Press, thanks to Matthew Davis and Sonya Unrein. I thank them also for making this book possible.

Thanks to the three visual artists who generously donated their work: Jim Franklin for the cover painting, Robert Bruce Warren Scott for photographing it, and Andrew Clark for the author photo.

Without naming names, I acknowledge a profound debt to my chosen masters, my teachers, and my colleagues all along the way, a debt that can be repaid only through generosity to other poets.

Finally, to my most faithful and knowing reader, Judy Lucas, who always sees in what is what could be.

for Henry, Brobear, Thos., Bobby D., Señor Reek,
Bartman, Walton, Richard, Zanko, Jim, & Brad

Contents

III. *Tyranny of Grasses*

IV. *Grace Given Back*

The difference between him and the other boys at such a time was that they knew it was make-believe, while to him make-believe and true were exactly the same thing.

—J. M. Barrie

I. The Half that Won't be Missed

Enact yourself between fixed points,
but loosely—let the wind anoint
clarity with death, and death with light.
Live on the sheerest opposites.

—Betty Adcock, "Four from the Spider"

THE GUN IN THE CHAIR

My first shot caught him cleanly
in the crease of his hip
as he lay on his side in a sniper's pose,
a crippling wound at the least, probably
death, if paintballs were bullets.
                                    I had chosen my moment,
ducked from the cover of warped plywood
nailed between aspens, and sprinted
through the close trees, crouching to pant
among the sagebrush of the open prairie.
Running hunched over the clasped gun,
I circled his position, pinned down as he was
by the pneumatic *thwap-thwap-thwap*
of my partner's fire.
                            I would like to say
I noted the Ming blue of the sky,
admired the patterning of the aspens,
their bark a creamy green khaki,
but instead I felt a quietly murderous joy.
    He was, is, my son.
I had not wanted to join in this game,
the current war raging and open-ended,
he nearly of age. How could I be sure
he would know the difference I just
had forgotten? He and his buddies
cajoled me, but it was I who chose to play.
                                    After all,

I had seen the gun, known to see it,
in the broken-off chair leg, its tapered foot
a nozzle, the two spindles, hacked short
with my father's saw, spaced just right
for machine-gun handles, and I knew
how to make that sound with my tongue
like bursts of rattle-snake mojo,
then yell, "I got you, you're dead!"
                                    I would like to say

I yelled it once more when I saw
the unnatural splatter—pink blood!—
in the crease of his hip where he lay,
but the down vest crumpled there
softened the impact so that for an instant
he did not register the hit, as happens
to some in the heat of battle,
and I, I chose instead

                  to shoot him again
this time on the skin of his arm,
the welt a red-rimmed crater days after.

If I could understand why I did that
we might do without war.

                      I would like to say
paintballs are only paintballs
not bullets, but then
the chair would be only the chair.

FIRST FALL

I horsed the largest rock, a slab of Colorado sandstone, up
to the crease of my hip like a baker's pan and duck-walked it
around the newly sunken and brimming garden pond, dropped it
into place, lipping over the rim so the fountain's runnel
would slide down its back and plummet—if "plummet" applies
to a six-inch drop—into the pool with a sound like wind chimes.

I stepped the second stone up the burm to form a shelving terrace,
a little bit of the Appalachian streams of boyhood transplanted
to the Buffalo-grass prairie of middle age. The third stone sat
at the brow of my molehill, hard to level. Spraddling the rise,
I hunched from the waist forward to wedge flaked-off slivers
of rock under the downhill edge, just a little bit...farther...under...

and I fell. Somersaulted like a codger checking his bumhole for fleas—
keel over smokestack, trivet over teakettle, workers over bosses,
stand back, folks, don't try this at home, the circus has come to town—
landing, briefly, coccyx first, on the second terrace, one instant there
of purest, self-dissolving vertigo, the order of the universe suspended,
drifting toward the ether, but, instead, I completed the natural arc,

plummeting head-first into the pond. I was awake then. I remembered
what I had forgotten: falling down. Decades since my last skinned knee,
half a century since looking back between my legs this head—a third
of my bodyweight then—toppled me. Falling was back, now, I knew,
for the duration. Silly man, I said, you bomb down black-diamond slopes,
yes, but the ice on the drive, the soap in the bath, they quietly slipped on

their new gravity. I remembered one of those best Sundays of childhood
floating the Sequatchie, our canoes bucking through the walled gorges
of white-capped rapids, the river broadening then, the water sheeting
by pastures of briefly curious cows. At the steep, muddy bank of the take-out
a boy come from church in white shirt and polished black shoes stood
looking down at us with envy, and my brother said, "Naw, it ain't slick."

In an instant, he knew where the slippery slope lies. He was awake then,
he who believed that man is born fallen, who believed in sin washed
away by baptism. I want to tell him, it takes more work than that, it takes
learning over and over. I want to tell him the child shows the man
how to stand, the man shows the child how to fall. I want to testify
to the causes that follow the effects. We must rise that we may fall.

FALLING OFF THE VICARIOUS

Past the dive shops dangling masks and snorkels,
the dreadlocked Rastas hawking joints to tourists,
we turn west at the Sandbox Beach Bar and Grill—
"No shirt, No shoes,
                              No problem"—and saunter
across the island's midriff, pausing to study
a glassless Land Rover squatting on it hubs,
vestigial of British Honduras, now Belize.
Beside each slab and plywood stilt-house,
a barrel cistern fed by a marble-run of gutters,
a bougainvillea sprung up from its leak:
a sustainable geometry. At the one store we stop
for a hand-recapped pint of local rum
and two Coca-Colas, one for the rum,
one for my son, who's not allowed caffeine at home.
The dock's tropical decking xylophones out
toward the anchored catamarans of the rich,
rich being relative. So we sit on the dock and drink,
watch a family of kids, one in each size,
diving for bottles—ours too now—the feel
of the water like emerging from sleep making love.
The rum was labeled "Extra Strong." My son
seems to be enjoying the caffeine of laughter,
the ducking and the being ducked. Now I'm the hoist
in the factory of splash, boosting them up to the end
of the dock so the next biggest one can sumo
them off, or the wirier one suddenly step round,
pivot on the hinge of the other's force, leave him
teetering there, a flung statue, flapping
to regain the perch, kicking off to clear the pilings.
This dance observes an etiquette: the matching
by size, the not holding on if the other might graze
a plank's edge, but a little voice whispers
Someone's going to get hurt, while another says,
Not yet, not yet, and with luck not badly.

My son squeezes a plump girl's laughter,
which he cannot budge, and suddenly I feel myself
pivot on the hinge of Coke and rum, rich and poor,
British and Belizean, force and finesse, and then
I fall off:

        Nothing's missing from this world,
nothing's hidden either. The sun impales
its yoke on the mast of a catamaran. After all,
where in this country would you hide, disguise, dump,
or bury a defunct Land Rover? Best leave it
where it stalled, in plain view, and walk on.

RESTLESS

And there arrives a lull in the hot race
Wherein he doth for ever chase
That flying and elusive shadow, rest.

—Matthew Arnold, "The Buried Life"

It's not that I'm without rest, it seems,
But that I don't want any, migrating
From the sofa and the newsless paper
To the chair and the book and back again.

It's not even all I've failed to finish
Or start, not the unanswered letters,
Stiff little sentinels of guilt. Not
The abandoned books like dead birds

Splayed face down on every table.
Not the leak that's turning the shelf
Beneath the sink to an oatmeal swag,
Nor the gutter so clogged it bleeds

A tannic plasma each time it rains,
Though, I admit, the piles festering
In the domestic subconscious of garage
And desk are sufficient to distraction.

On my third snack-raid this hour, I hear
My mother's voice chiding from the center
Of another summer Sunday afternoon:
"Boredom is a lack of imagination!"

Well, it's not that, Mom, but the lack
Of direction, because when I imagine
It's all that I'm not doing, and,
When I do it, it's not what I imagined.

Nothing for it but to keep on trudging
Until the compass needle spins at the Pole,
All headings then equivocally equal,
No choice but to bed the snow and rest.

THE ART OF BUILDING A FIRE

Why cram the car with mildewed gear
and drive for hours up a road that pretzels
and turns to teeth-rattling washboard
just to stake a patch of human geometry,
squat beside a smoking fire, sip bad coffee,
and watch fingers of sunlight angling steeper
down through fir and aspen branches, as if
there isn't loneliness enough in life?

That summer I hitched north from the Carolinas,
sleeping tucked up under the overpasses,
set on hiking the Appalachian Trail
back from the White Mountains, and walked away
from that New Hampshire spire and two-pump station
to begin the trek up the first shrug of mountain,
the trees closed ranks around me, the mineral dark
honed a crystalline edge in the air, and I—

no other way to say it—fled those mountains
to sleep with my knees pressed to the dash
of a strange El Dorado hurtling south.
This clambering one moment to be let out,
whimpering the next to sit on the lap—
it banks my fire, rolls out my downy chrysalis;
it hoards the trove of embers, rubies phasing
to emeralds and back on every breath,

but hankers for the fiddle and the passed jug.
It leads me here alone then leaves me stewing
memories of those it was I meant to leave.
And what it loves is not the sky's
symphonic gestures, nor the mountain's grand
indifference, nor even the intimacies
of the creek-side glen, the stream's
fugued shushings, but the tent,

it loves the tent, that breathing membrane,
and loves it best when the wind pops the fly
like a spinnaker, and the rain pummels
and sizzles an arm's length above your face,
but you dare not reach up and touch it,

lest it come in, so lie still in a darkness
nearly complete and listen, listen harder,
draw closer your swaddling, your winding,

drink in the nearness of the distance,
mingling so equally gratitude with dread,
until the breath you had not known you held
lets go, and you breathe with it.
The way a fire is made less from kindling
or timber or even the flame you strike
than air, the trick to arrange not logs but gaps.

WATERMELON

When we "watch" a film in the theater, we actually spend as much as fifty percent of the time in darkness, with the projector's shutter closed and nothing before us on the screen.
          —David Cook, A History of Narrative Film

The hill's grasses flattened in trails
where we bowled ourselves in the barrel:
back rounded, feet braced, knees hugged,
portholes to left and right revolving
around the tree line's axis blue
green blue green blue green blue
enough to make the mind wander...

    *The way living is punctuated only
    by intermittent atolls of lucidity,
    the rest spent coasting the vast
    connective ocean of distraction
    and day-dream, sleep and reverie.*

Where the barrel comes to rest
I unfold my legs. The sun's plumb bob
wobbles beneath me, sends me
stumbling over clods, tipsy partner
to the scarecrow in the Jackson's garden.
There, in seaweed-fingered camouflage,
prehistoric eggs line the furrows...

    *The way a corner turned in the mind
    might suddenly cast the familiar
    as a dazzling, unforeseen sign
    of our alien status in the world
    we have come so fastidiously to ignore.*

A maternity ward of melons
nested among pubic vines,
dusty, smooth, sun-warmed,
the one I lift cool beneath,
dense as a fresh piglet, its
perfect print retained in the dirt,
trailing a twist of cord I snap...

The way each moment's replete
with choice as with chance, the script
opening onto myriad endings,
each gap a portal to a different life,
till the lights strike us dumb in our seats.

Standing before Mrs. Jackson's door,
a thief, otherwise, mother said,
I admit, I admit, but only give back
the rind, whole and seamless once more.
The comb of water's flesh,
the magazine of glass-smooth pips,
the tacky elixir of flamingo nectar

I keep, the half that won't be missed.

BOUNDARIES OF SEEING

—for Judy

The temptation is to watch the clouds,
    swollen with moonlight, drift
  across the night sky, a migrating

herd of leviathans, but if
    you lie spread open on the earth
  long enough and focus

between them, you may see
    the clouds slow, the obsidian
  depth behind them ease

into motion, and sense yourself,
    in a parallel gesture, begin
  to accelerate, until like

the twin runners of a dogsled,
    you and the night sky
  are reeling along the luminous track

of frozen cloud. Once,
    white men trundled a projector
  over the tundra, as only

white men would do,
    and splashed a movie across
  the igloo's breath-sheened wall:

black-and-white people raced
    to and fro, making
  overblown gestures to make up

for the lack of sound. What
    did they see, the Eskimos,
  polite enough to feign a chuckle

when the visitors slapped their knees
    and, when the film came
  flapping to a halt, to praise

the shifting abstract patterns, how
    with such slow grace they swam
  across the igloo's starry dome,

like the breath of the Aurora,
    they said, in the cupped
  hands of the night sky.

SLIDES OF THE FIELD TRIP
(or, "The Overwintering Ecology of a Tropical Species")

Here's the road-weary team in the Sierra Chincuas.
The white Econovan disgorges lawn chairs
And computers, skillets, guitars, and atomic scales,
Cases of toilet rolls and a machine engineered
For the gradual freezing of monitored butterflies.

Here's a sun-drenched valley inside a paperweight.
Someone's shaken it, and ragged piebald flakes
Litter the sky all the way to the Caribbean. And look,
Someone's woven a breathing raiment, iridescent
Paisleys in ebony and gold, and with it draped

This corner of the forest, tucking every contour.
Have you heard the one about the flock of birds
Hovering in the shape of a tree, the winged leaves
Rustling with their own breeze, and the hunter,
Sure he'd seen birds just moments before

Scratches his head and trudges home over the hill?
And here, in the researcher's dream, she approaches,
Bare skin powdered with a crystalline dust
The shade of snapdragons, sweet on his tongue
As confectioner's sugar. Spread now above him,

Her wings are stained-glass windows hinged
At his groin, moonlight batiking the forest floor.
In closing, the graphed data suggest body-water
Is hazardous, hastening the onset of the "freezing event"—
Its measurable burst of heat the soul's release.

A DAY'S OUTING

...think of him as uninjured, barely disturbed.

—Elizabeth Bishop, "Little Exercise"

Think of them drawing away from the rental dock,
parting outboard fumes, vagrant ducks,
the promised sun not yet up.

Think how they round the river's final bend,
the boat bridling where the current meets the tide,
and front the salt-thickened wind.

The crooked trail of markers, each unplumbed
by harsher weather, tended by its gull
or pelican, leads to open water.

See how the bar's mottled sand rises into view
between the ragged coast and the shrimp boats
sprigging the horizon like hors d'oeuvres,

as if the tide's folds had been drawn back
to reveal a shoulder, a scallop of hip—
private cays to castle and shell.

But the tide has flooded now, the V of sand,
where once the unminded boat's prow
was wedged, is washed away.

Listen to the helicopter's faint drumming, step out
onto the balcony, and see the tiny floodlight
shudder across black water.

Think, then, of the tide's run portward, the inlet
gorged at sunset; think of them returning,
only weary, slightly burned.

BLACK PATTERN ON A MOCHA GROUND

If not "quick as a snake," then quick enough
    I bring the brick's end down
On his head in one tamping motion. But that
        Cliché is wrong: snakes take life

Slowly, depending more on camouflage,
    The failed perception of others, than speed.
Bud, a big black man whose bad heart
        Sent bolts down his arm, told me

The thing scared him most in Nam
    Wasn't "gooks or bombs" but a cobra,
Hood flared, reared belt-high,
        Parting a column of soldiers on a dusty road

Faster than a man could run. Bud
    Lashed the air with his arm to show me,
The arm that later that summer,
        Laying bricks, struck his heart.

There is a distinction between aggression
    And self-defense we fail to grant
To snakes. Lost on Bud, it was not
        Lost on the Vietcong. A summer before,

The war raging beyond the edges of my
    Perception, I hiked Chilhowie Mountain,
Stopping to eat a half-pack of *Fig Newtons*
        In the unmanned fire tower on top.

In all directions, the green canopy,
    Beneath which, hiking down, I caught
An ancient black snake and fed him
        Into the sleeve of my shirt. I tell you,

All the clichés are wrong.
    Smooth and dry as talcum,
He wound around my heart three times,
        And, further down the slope, lent me

Nerve to trap an arm-thick rattler
  With a forked stick, slide my hand
Up behind the flanges of its skull, and carry it—
    Mouth sprung—to the nature center's terrarium.

I am not a snake, nor am I a Vietcong.
  Even so, neither can I understand
The failed perception by which
    My neighbor, or his teenage son,

Swerved to hit or did not swerve
  To miss the snake crossing our road.
His perfect tube is ruptured: a yellow
    Loop of intestine hangs out,

A staggered pattern of obsidian chips
  Floats the mocha ripples on his back,
And I, coils around my heart,
    Bring the brick down hard.

THE MOUNTAIN LION AT BEAR CREEK ARCHERY
(with a line and a half stolen from d. h. lawrence)

At Bear Creek Archery, mounted high
        above the cash register and the glass case
where razor-winged broadhead points gleam
        like futuristic fighter planes,
stands a big cat the color of sandy boulders
when the sun is high, or the color of shadows
        between sandy boulders when the sun is low.

Posed in defiance of an unseen foe, her face
        is pulled back into a kind of mask
baring the teeth, and she raises (or has had raised)
        one forepaw, claws extended, fine claws
rooted in the bone and coming to a sudden hook.
The woman behind the counter wears fatigues
        and bristles a short-cropped Mohawk.

The pose suggests a moment's recognition
        at the last, an inevitable meeting of equals,
a facing opponent who matched her fierceness
        with his own. She peers above
the racks of cammo and blaze-orange clothing,
the pendant display of arrows split by arrows,
        macraméd like a Sioux's bone breastplate,

And the walls hung-round with bows, enough to arm
        a back-to-wilderness militia. But theirs is not
the wilderness of longbows—leather gripped, sinew strung,
        dangling spotted turkey feathers—
theirs are compound bows, rigged with pulleys
like shrimp-boat tackle or spa machines to multiply
        a man's strength. This does not concern her.

Perched on the nubs of broken pine limbs, she hisses—
        or I hear her hiss—at the backs of archers
trained on the brightly lit end of the gallery.
        They are stout, serious, silent men,
their arrow paths signaled by a humming thwack,
punctuated in a second split by a hollow *tock*.
        They can shoot the pupil out of any eye.

For a moment, an archaic feeling. I am not a man
          like these, the only animal in the world
to fear. I could envy their single-minded
               sureness, their unlovely machinery's
guarantee, but I do not want to own her death—
what a gap in the world!—and know the pose
          for the lie it is. She pads

through new snow, late winter sunlight
          sifting down through spruce bows like snow,
and threads a stand of aspen, the bark stitched on
               with black thread. Then a sudden leap,
mad thrashing on the ground...stillness again.
Panther, painter, cougar, puma, catamount,
          you who never feared our unseen foe.

AT THE PILAR YACHT CLUB

Rafting guides swagger in bananaed cowboy hats or sashay
In cat-eye shades, then pack their vans with eager
And doughy gringos, headed down the Rio Grande.
It's like that here in Pilar.

Across the highway, the tan shoulders of the Sangre de Cristos
Hump into sunlight delicious as clarified butter.
Tri-colored pickups wiffle all day from Santa Fe to Taos.
It's like that here, in Pilar.

Now a squadron of hummingbirds copters the verandah. Pairs swish
And flare opalescent skirts, circling *paso doble* mid-air
As they vie for the feeders, cursing in fast-forward Spanish.
It's like that, here in Pilar.

Ambling in late for double expressos and Frieda's killer burritos,
A rancher in sandals, a Navajo biker, a tie-dyed girl with a cur
On a string, swapping the regular's banter with Rico.
It's like, you know, that, here in Pilar.

Now the metal roof ticks each ascending degree. Only, listen:
The waves of ancient seas returning pulsate a hollow roar
With the planet's warming. We wait for our sails to stiffen.
Yes, it's like that here in Pilar.

HILLBILLY ZEN

"Hurry ev'ry chanst you get," Tom said,
a near smile on his face I couldn't decipher.
I was fifteen, come to live in his woods
for the summer, rising from my tent at dawn
to hold the plumb bob steady as I could
at the end of the hundred-foot survey chain
Tom pulled to a vibrating stillness between us.

I loved best the clear voice of the machete
ringing one note from a sliced oval of sapling
like a bell that calls the world to contemplation.
I understood the harder substance hones.
There, the file's whiskers of steel, glinting,
the pleasure in mastery of a pure machine.
One day, sharpening a benchmark stake, I sliced

a clean line instantly jeweled with crimson beads
down the outside of my pinky finger,
opening like a snap-bean to the bone.
"Yep, you done it now," was all Tom said.
It was a kind of holiday, the switch-back drive
off the mountain down to the valley's clinic.
Shouldered between Reb and Bud in the back,

I forgot about my finger as the beater Chevy
swung each outside curve toward the yawning valley
and Tom, one-handing the wheel, craned around
to tell of running 'shine on moonless nights.
I could hear, still can hear, the bored-out cylinders
roaring down the gap, see the cop's headlights
swinging bend to bend in the rearview mirror.

I top a rise, kill my lights, and cut the engine,
drop down into an over-grown logging road.
That moment there, sitting in the pitch black,
listening to the engine tick, no hurry, no hurry
at all. The Fury cruiser cannonballs past,
fades. The hillbilly Zen of wiliness
bred to ease. It took me 35 years, Tom.

II. Unchecked Liberties

I saw how the night came,
Came striding like the color of the heavy hemlocks.
I felt afraid.
And I remembered the cry of the peacocks.

—Wallace Stevens, "Domination of Black"

NO. 9 BLUFF VIEW

was a Victorian pastiche:
pitched roof slated,
brick arches keystoned,
outside features outsized
for the tiny rooms and too steep
switch-back stairs. Upstairs,
Dad knocked out the ceiling,
swung a porch swing on chains
from exposed rafters, wrapped
a loft around the new
walk-in kitchen.
Down four flights,
the "boy's dorm": two sets
of steel bunks abutting
the coal-bin, the fireplace's
grate and fender like the cowl
of a dwarf locomotive, driving
a clawed, ensanguined shadow
through the fir-tree forest
of our winter nights.

Across the street, the Hunter
Gallery's Corinthian columns
surveyed the broad Tennessee
from the high bluffs it
had carved. The sloping lawn
stopped short at the shear
drop to the river, guarded
by a wrought-iron fence
with tines like arrows. At night,
arc lights set
in the lawn made the columns
loom upward, motorists
squinting from the far bank
as we strutted before the footlights
scenes adopted loosely
from *Star Trek* or *Hamlet*,
our shadows striding vastly
among the spectral columns.

We were omnipotent in the most
fragile sense. They
allowed us that, our mutual
stepparents upstairs grooving
as José Feliciano lit
their fire, or Otis went
FA fa fa fa fa FA FA fa fa,
while we four raided the cellar
of wine for which we'd worn
grape-stain anklets:
Hamburger Red, and the white
dubbed *Tawny Murk.*

Lovers parking in the Hunter's
lot required "observation"
by "military advisers"—words
we'd picked up from snatches
of foreign correspondent chatter,
in the background, "sporadic fire."
We didn't mind black
neighbors, or making a buck
on the white gentry's flight
to higher ground until
they invaded us with dozers,
dropped a freeway on our village,
unzipped the familiar staircase
from its balusters, ruptured the chimney's
blackened larynx, spilling
a century of chalky bricks.
We lobbed them grenade fashion,
playing Army in the rubble,
windows exploding in splinters
of sunlight, nearly blinding
our closest enemy, until
one of us bled real blood
all the way to the *Emergency.*

Nights stretched on the Hunter's
lawn we sometimes heard
eerie music waft
up from the water, lyrics
confused among echoes

off of the bluff. Below,
a tiara of lights inched
upstream, its paddlewheel plowing
a vanishing milky furrow.
Transfixed by tiny couples
dancing the upper deck,
we leaned on the tips of arrows.

MOUNTAIN GATHERING

—for Nat Swann

In winter, the sky slatey,
   the Oconaluftee is lead-hued
and flows with the swiftness of snow-melt.

Dapple-gray stones, slick
   as snake eggs, beg touch,
but soon you rise with hands that ache.

Where Chasteen Creek forks,
   a clach of homestead apples grows
more gnarly each unharvested season—

arthritic branches calibrate
   the closeness of the cove. There the trail
rabbits down through a laurel tunnel

to the log bridge, a span
   of hickory trunk adzed flat.
Pause, test its spring, look up

at the part in the trees, until
   the braiding water's roar swells
suddenly too close and shoos you across.

The trail's ascent begins
   where Richland Mountain's shoulder slopes
to water, winding up in switchbacks

along the contour lines.
   The children bolt ahead, flag,
are passed by their granddad, his admonition,

"Rhythm, steady rhythm."
   For you too now each step is placed,
the heat spent to check a fall, recover

stride from a slick root,
   waste. When sky shows through
the hatch-work of trunks along the ridgeback,

each bend promises
    to be the last. The sky opens,
  the valley spreads, and Fiery Dragaman's

skein of pipe smoke
    twines with pewter wisps of cloud
  blowing through Newfound Gap. Descent

is quick. In the bottoms
    an unexpected clearing proves
  a settler's graveyard. The flu of '96,

that winter's heavy snow,
    the doctor, such as he was, three
  days by wagon, the parents' nights of riding

a child's tattered breath
    in and out of turbid dreams
  ends with wailing, here, in this clearing,

where the stones dwindle
    like bars of soap, barely legible,
  soon not: *James   Monroe   Finley*

Rest   with   Angels, also
    his siblings Edward and Betheme,
  two Wiggins, four Silers, three Ketchams,

and a stone faun with legs
    folded under. The children test
  the spring of held silence long enough

to notice gravestones make
    good climbing. The loop closes
  back at the campground's temporary settlement,

the fire that waits to be pondered
    or worried with sticks, the whiskey drunk
  or marshmallows squandered, the stories told

or hearkened to,
    the mummy bags filled sooner
  or later, according to age, earned either way

by walking a mile per year or a mile per decade.

DAYS-O'-WORK

We slipped the campfire's halo on pretense,
crunched through new snow to the bathhouse,
warmed by spirals of livid orange wire,
and held between us the plug of tobacco
we'd sneaked from the top dresser drawer
it shared with old Army brass and rubbers.
There, wrapped in cellophane, jacketed

with uncured leaf as soft as moleskin,
was the length of all those summer days,
all of that sun fused in the seed,
erupting in plumes of leaves, broad
and floppy as cavalier hats or magician's
handkerchiefs, unfurling skyward to clustered
sprays of small white flowers in the fall.

And all of that care, all of those hands
to bind the stems like teepee poles,
to hang the bunches in tiers, to fire
the smoker, to bale the leathery bounty
for the cutting floor, for pipe tobacco
first, then cigarettes, until what's left
is stirred with molasses or licorice, extruded

in planks, chopped into plugs, wrapped.
There, too, all of the days that I
would chew up, all of the Latin
I'd fail to learn, chewing, the quid
dropping silently from my tongue's tip
into the *Coke* can's hole, and all,
the Faulkner I'd read—"He ejaculated

a bullet of chocolate saliva"—as well
as all the nails of all the days
I hammered, chewing, then all the desks
beside which sat the brass spittoon
or the antique porcelain one, its rim
chipped in a brawl in a saloon, or so
I imagined, plus all the imagining it took

to get me through the work I thought
I had to do and thoughtlessly did,
working to chew and chewing to love
the work of being a man. I quit
only after all addictions but work
had worn themselves out in me.
Having come to live again in the South,

I drive the county two-lanes past field
upon field of broad, bright leaves—
magnificent that plant!—and, in the fall,
the storied barns, their lower doors
opening on wardrobes of fairy's gowns,
beggar's tatters, widow's weeds,
struck golden by late sun

angling through the frames. Stuck again
behind a wood-railed farm truck,
one of the legion headed for warehouses,
each overloaded with over-stuffed bales
swaddled in canvas like leaves to be burned,
I listen to news of tobacco legislation
and think of my students' Reynolds scholarships,

their fourth-generation small farms,
their family's tithe of a crop that pays
four times any other. I walk
from my house through woods by moonlight
to witness the fields of sighing leaves
and feel their breath. I wake choking,
my hand to my mouth to pull out wad

upon wad of chaw that keep retching
up from my throat, black as cancer.
Lying then in the dark, I see
the bathhouse window's wash of light on the snow
and hear my brother in the other stall
gagging with the laughter of a man surprised
to find himself in the body of a boy.

BLIND JEFF DEATH REVISITS #3 CLARK ROAD

If I follow the bread crumbs not away but back
        into the forest
toward the wee queer house nestled in shadow
        beneath the pines,
I see smoke from wood I chopped braiding upward
        and hear John Fahey's
"Dance of the Inhabitants of the Palace of King Philip
        XIV of Spain"
chiming wavily, like a guitar down a well, on the turntable
        I hung from the rafters
because each step or closing door quaked the foundation,
        framed, as it was,
with war-time nails and clad in scaly, puce,
        asbestos.

If I peek in at the bathroom window, the rattling
        panes spangled
with breath frost, I see myself seated there
        on the toilet lid
wearing the overalls that were my uniform, the thick
        cowhide moccasins
the indigent giant I gave leave to camp in the grove
        hand-made for me,
holding the syringe up to the bulb like an offering,
        flicking out
bubbles of air—Oh, even to watch the needle
        slide in,
the red poppies blossoming in the barrel, the eyelids
        drift down
and head float back against the wall, is to taste
        in my teeth
that bitterness, to feel the body becoming the only
        me I am,
the blood of the womb the blood of me...
        I pull away,

Eddy around the corner past the stolid sow
        of the kerosene tank,
and stop by the bedroom window as its frames
        unreel me
drifting in and out of focus with leading ladies
        Central Casting
keeps changing, though the scene is always
        love and lust
laboring toward union, falling back into difference.

        (And, too, the years
of nights I drew close the mother-sewn quilts,
        willing against gravity
to flit between the closing ranks of trunks or
        soar above
the bombed crowns of twilit buildings, fleeing
        a hooded figure
or my familiar, the tiger, who'd turn the corner
        of chalet or tenement
to stop me in the midst of unrelated action, watch
        almost sadly,
I think, until I shook myself into flight—
        Where has she gone?)

Curling about the fourth corner to close
        this blessing round,
I'm drawn up short before that dripping
        February predawn,
Charlotte not long given to the ground,
        the day before
fed spoon by cooked spoon into the vein,
        each speed-ball rush
and refracting implosion of light in the brain
        diminished
by the previous jolt, the glutting frequency,
        the boosted dose,
night drawing the curtains, bolting the doors,
        rechecking the locks

that could not keep out or in the cocaine-fused
          amalgam of
abandonment, grief, and adolescent dread,
          which finally boiled
demons from the corners in soot-black smoky spirals,
          hissing and gnashing,
until I fled, commando-crawled the sopping bushes
          with a Bowie knife
clenched in my teeth and came back shivering for one
          last fix:

It snapped my head back, set the piston of my heart
          jolting against the ribs,
plugged the spidery harness of my nerves into a
          shorting circuit,
arms and legs jerking like a manic puppet's,
          wrenching a hernia
I clung so hard to the kitchen sink's enameled lip
          not to fall,
then convulsed toward light in the arms-out walk
          of Frankenstein's Creature:

*If only I could master these hands, grasp and turn
          this knob,*
I would be free, just then looking up to see
          a white figure
step from the curls of mist onto the concrete stoop.
          He's come,
I think, *to take me,* and pause for him to open
          the door, the door
through which he only peers at me, sadly
          I think, as if
he's come to tell me something and chosen to wait,
          to wait for me
to live through this and join him there one day
          when I'll need it more.

MELOS, THE USUAL

One minute it's eggs sizzling,
the minuet of packing lunches,
  searching the hamper

for socks, the dishwasher
steaming to be unloaded, and then
  it's who gets

the silverware *my turn you always I never*
I hate you: the family unraveling
  to music

the claustrophobia of inescapable
relations. Violins better not get
  pizzicato, that's when

he breaks the screen-door, she flings
herself, a rag-doll, across the bed—
  so predictable no one

saw it coming or could resist. Always afterwards,
the remorse: delicious. He didn't really
  mean it, the father,

standing over the son to love him with
ridicule and leashed violence. *What*
  got into where'd that

come from—like a manic player piano
jolted into helter-skelter
  ragtime, unloosed hooligans

bashing heads? Oh, the ineluctable seduction of—
Duck!—*watch your head!* A match
  flares against clammy stone, the vault

of archaic scripts unscrolling at their feet—*Quick now!*
the curse must be translated, Son,
  hold that torch steady, damn it!

The fate of the world may depend
on what transpires here
  in this close chamber.

ALL THE CONNECTIONS

Today, coalition forces drop bombs on...
Serbians, tomorrow, perhaps Afghanis.
   In the essay I may not live to write,

I'd show them all the connections in Washington.
Today, a pair of teenagers in Colorado
   went to school with homemade bombs—

screaming like ethnic cleansers, they
blew the faces off of their enemies.
   That essay, it might get published in *Mother Jones*,

and lefties everywhere would nod, though it would bomb
among the men who run Congress,
   so busy guarding the home fires in Washington

for LockheedBoeingRockwellRaytheon.
Meanwhile, in Kosovo or Colorado
   the pieces of faces float down to earth

like the shreds of essays Afghani teenagers
may not live to make at home.
   Today, the National Rifle Association

said teenagers must be protected from bullies,
not bullets, no, that's not it,
   guns must be protected from teenagers, or,

now I've got it, more guns must be issued
to protect future teenagers
   whose faces may float down in shreds of static

across the screens of every TV in America.
Today, the TV men tell us, with close-up
   footage of faces going off in Washington,

that Serbian, Afghani—or was it Iraqi?—
teenagers should switch off their essays
   on TV violence before they blow up

faces inside every Congressman in America.
Meanwhile, in news today from Wall Street,
   the shreds of teenage Iraqi faces

rain down like tickertape in the canyons of Manhattan,
and the bulls and the bears shall lie down together
  like the bullies and the pall bearers. That essay,

the one I may not live to write,
would show them how the bombs not yet
  going off in Washington just might

be connected to the homemade bombs set
to go off inside every teenager in America.
  After all, bombs do not kill people,

just enemies, and Congressmen do not make bombs,
and TVs do not shred faces anymore
  than SerbiAfghaniIraqi teenagers

become the last best hope of the National
Rifle Association simply by being
  the targets of bombs made right here at home

by LockheedBoeingRockwellRaytheon.
Which is precisely the point that Afghani, Iraqi,
  or perhaps, next time, Iranian teenagers

might get their faces shredded for daring to see.
I swear to you, they'd see all the connections
  as clearly as I do in Washington

if only they'd read the homemade essays
Iraqi teenagers may not live to write
  simply by blowing up in our faces.

THE MAN AT (NOT ON) THE DUMP

> *Could it after all*
> *Be merely oneself, as superior as the ear*
> *To a crow's voice?*
>
> —Wallace Stevens

No bone yard for cast-off images
or worn metaphysical fabliau, just
an industrial dumpster, gray paint

dinged with bleeding stars of rust,
its pneumatic compacting plate poised
to mash a Wal-Mart visit's

ecologically disastrous packaging, the tireless
trike, its skewed handlebars, and,
who knows, the mattresses of the dead.

The sign says, "NO BUILDING OR YARD
REFUSE," which is exactly what I have,
4:50 on a Saturday, the full bed

of a loaner pick-up, rain beginning
to ping the corrugated tin roof
of the attendant's pill-box shed.

A gray-whiskered leprechaun
fumbles in his overalls, and I can see
this will not be a rushable context, so lean

on the cab, feel my way toward beg
or bribe. He squints, reckons he can take
a bit of it, waves me back, and steps

round my side to check the load, I think.
"You know," he hisses, "I wouldn't tell this
to just anybody, but I been doin it

since I was twelve, us kids was put
to bed on the screen porch, my cousin—
she was thirteen—and me shared

a bed, she had just a couple blonde hairs
down there, and it was sweet."
Shoveling rotten timber from the bed,

wondering when he might stop me unloading,
I say "I'll bet it was," which is all he needs
to keep on going, so I do too,

at his pace, slow, adding "Sure enough"
or "Oh yeah?" when he wants me to,
shooting a shrapnel of bent nails

into the dumpster with a broom, a fallout
of pink insulation wisps, then using
his long-handled dustpan to tidy

the pavement where I've spilled, as he
avers, "I like the taste of that
pickled peach," his eyes badger-fierce

as he palms the compactor button. "Uh huh,"
is all I have left, leaning on the cab now,
faking it, not wanting to cut him off

before he finishes, driven finally
to leave him there gesticulating to the rain.
Driving past the shabbily festive

trailer park, which next year's flood will
sweep away, the boat ramp that disappears
into the hog-runoff-brown of the *Tar*,

I glimpse the moon climbing through trees
strewn with bits of high-water confetti
and reflect that Wallace Stevens also

was full of shit, because that, that
was a "philosopher's honeymoon," and I,
if disburdened, am far from purified.

WHAT IS

—for Gaston Caesar Raoul

As the plane slices through a chiffon stratum
      of cloud, a series of scarves drawn riffling
    across banked windows, I read

Chögyam Trungpa's *Cutting Through Spiritual*
      Materialism. Multi-armed bodhisattvas
    float mid-air on lotus blossoms, but we

bump through the cirrus washboard that makes
      Florida a hot destination for lightening
    and refuse to contemplate

what this mixture of speed and frailty
      might render. A sudden parting, and there
    "the ground," as if to say

the unity of all locations, its sturdy
      greens and browns, the material
    materialized from the ethereal: "Surrendering

does not involve preparing for a soft
      landing; it means just landing
    on hard, ordinary ground. Once

we open ourselves, then we land
      on what is." In a flash I foresee
    the coming weekend's reunion: the petty

disappointment in friends who have aged, cocktails
      commencing at noon, ending on the back
    of a convertible howling down boulevards

of harlequin palms, the multiple marriages
      we've shared in heart-felt confidence
    blending to slurs on lost omnipotence

in meat-market bars. Looking up,
      I see lightening fork the plane,
      the instruments cascading sparks, a fractal

blossoming of flames bear forth
>   *Sengá Dra-dog*, the terrible protector,
>   his tusked grimace and necklace of skulls,

"He who teaches with the lion's roar
>   that subdues the heretics of hope and fear."
>   We rally outside of baggage claim,

cling to one another for a moment there
>   on the hard, ordinary ground, resplendent
>   with speed and frailty, no flight from suffering.

STORIES THAT BECOME US

"He came in early and ordered the usual..."
or so tradition begins one story.
The crowd swelled by nine, lingerers
and serious drinkers eyeing each other
above the rows of bottles, partnering
for the music that strikes up at ten.

What you can count on is tradition here:
haloed brass, elbow-worn oak, stories
that become us in the retelling.
If you tell a sad story in a bar,
people will laugh, and you
must feel better.

On either side of the gleaming register,
beneath the glass reflecting glass,
identical fish tanks cast a green pallor.
One holds an arrangement
of finger-sized shad, the other
a lone, hand-sized fish that sulks

in the depths of fluorescent half-light,
a bulldog-of-a-fish with jutting jaw.
Same size ponds, different perspectives.
The small fish all shift together
like pieces in a mobile stirred by the breeze
of our overlapping conversations.

The woman next to me, who tells me
she's 35 and divorced,
is transfixed, her eyes glazed
like a TV watcher's glimpsed
through an open window at night.
The barkeep has a little net.

In one motion he dips a small fish
and plops it in with the big guy—
Bam!—like a mousetrap, one bite.
The whole bar goes up an octave.
The woman is horrified, on the verge
of public protest, so I try

to calm her and her divorce
with college talk of the natural
order, dog eat dogma. The loss
you can describe to a stranger
is equal to the distance
between you. Everyone orders another,

while the South American wonder
hovers with half-mast eyes,
rotating in his holy light
like the hand of a Tai Chi master.
We who by that death are now one
work our way through rounds

and the worn catalog
of broken-down traditions
by which we are broken,
the telling as the breaking
now part of the tradition.
The band warms up its engines,

the mirror empties toward the dance floor,
and, for a moment, I sit alone beside her.....
"...and as he reached the door
and looked back, she slapped
the bar and said, 'The fish,
feed the fish, feed the fish.'"

IN JENNY-LYNN'S GARDEN

After warm-up chat and frosty
                    Margaritas
and children shushed off to children's things,
I stroll out the back kitchen door and find
on the island of lawn
                    a plumped pillow
beneath the canopy of Oriental Magnolia:

angular branches, indigo sky,
blossoms big
                    as saucers, white
with pinkish edges, float
                    above
like candles borne on origami boats.
I am
        at the bottom of something and do not
matter in the least. This dance of leaves
and branch tips—as orchestrated
                            as random—
breathes with the big breathing. I am
here,
        alive and well in a new city
once more, having slipped
those previous identities. Even so

distant frequencies rearrive
                    in waves
like a dialed Philco snagging channels
off the prairie:
                    there's the mammoth
plinking of the Good-Humor man,
the shush-shush
                    shush-shush
of sprinklers past dusk, a whistle
issued from a back stoop—
                    come home—
all coalescing
                    into a dimensional
                            feeling,

all the other moments like this one
lining up in jeweled relay,
connecting all the way back,
the switch
        thrown. But then, at once,

the revealed order of black vectors
reverts to power lines
        converging
on the house, and the ice-cream truck
runs over the laughing dog,
careening out of earshot like a released
balloon.
        Postmodern irony trumps
nostalgia every time. Even so,

after Jenny-Lynn comes out
to grill the salmon to manna, after
conversation
        fugues us for hours
of feasting like Icelanders, and even
after safe passage home
to the bed I know
        knows me,
the very anchor of my pillow
unmoors, falling
        skyward
           beautifully.

REASONS FOR LAWNS

If, having come to an alien shore possessed of the notion
that Nature waits only to be conquered or else will send
mammoth beasts for whom my flesh is a delicacy or men
whose skin dictates they peel mine, slowly, while roasting
another yet living part of me, then, yes, I could see
the impulse to clear as much space around me and mine
as can be hacked, stripped, razed, leveled, and barbered.

Still, I can't help but mourn those trees Charles Dickens
saw on his travels to the frontiers of America (meaning then
Missouri or Mississippi) into the hollowed-out stumps of which
he watched four men ride horses, nor but feel a loss smoldering
in those scenes he describes of forests felled and burning
from here to the horizon, the black haze more choking
than the mills of Manchester and Birmingham put together.

And I'd be willing to entertain the Spartan aesthetics
of those for whom gradations in shades of sand or limestone
from moon-pale to lavender are the source of a somber passion
and so honor the arid graces of Nevada and Arizona,
if not for the stunted corn and dry wells of Nogales,
the artery of the Colorado shunted just to water
the lawns and golf courses of Las Vegas and Phoenix.

And I admit a moment's sense of something akin to homage
whenever I drive past one of those hill-mounted houses,
their perfectly asymmetrical configurations of trees
and lawns sweeping down like lush Hibernian carpets
on which we the wee people might gladly curl and slumber,
and admit, as well, the moment following soon after
of a more belittling sense of something akin to envy.

But how am I to complain—having arrived at that dream
invented by the out-migrating burghers of London
of the country in the city, the city in the country,
removed from the workers while proximate to the gentry,
whom they were supplanting—if, each weekend morning,
a neighbor jerks a cord tied to my cerebral cortex
and sparks ignite, behind my eyes, an angry little engine?

And how can I, complicit, ignore the censorious head shakes
at the lolling of my seed-heads, the dreadlocks of my creepers,
or turn down next door's offer to lend me his old mower
and not then parade within range of all good neighbors
like a shooting-arcade buffalo, given time now to ponder
how the dream of frontiers prone to unchecked liberties became one
with a social order founded on the tyranny of grasses.

III. Tyranny of Grasses

Dreaming of how poignantly tragic my death
would seem, but, having thought about it,
I happily took myself into the darkness
of the underground, where I was king.

—Rodney Jones, "Beautiful Child"

BENEATH THE HOUSE FOUNDATIONS LIE

Intruder in the unstirred darkness, I come
with greetings for the King of the Spiders.
Obeisant beyond an infant's crawl, I hold
a continuous push-up, bellying the dirt.

Here, the residue of our lives has settled,
sifted down through the cracks of years
as a dust finer than 10x sugar,
welling in the lids of paint cans never

to be reopened, flouring the luggage
travel has outdistanced and all the gear
for failed or abandoned hobbies and sports.
Here is the border between *store* and *hide.*

And I would let it lie, heed the warning
of the taut web suddenly met, if not
for the unrelenting rain, the house
rain undercut last night just north

of us, toppled down the escarpment,
bedding mother and child under blankets
of mud, the father come home late.
So I gulp the mildew, suck the flashlight,

follow a trickle to the uphill footing
and find—the third little pig withstanding—
that a brick is only a stolid sponge,
that the little Dutch boy didn't stick

for loyalty or courage but because
he'd not outrun the burst dike's torrent.
Scuttling back toward light I glimpse
the huge, leggy shadow behind.

I PAINTED THE HOUSE MYSELF

As sleep is a form of work, so I
am the dull but diligent overachiever,
just trying to get it down in black

                      and white.
If I could, I'd lift from the myriad array
of postage-stamp-sized samples

                      the one named
Fiery Coral or *Bishop's Purple* or *Lime
Sherbet* and stoically say,
This one, fourteen gallons, please.

                      But, as it is,
innocuous *Basswood*, neither light nor dark,
neither brown nor gray, serving a certain
oyster logic—

            drab camouflage
for a lustrous opaline interior life—
must do.

    I'd thought *Sans Souci*
was just the name of a raunchy bar on 9th
until I crossed the Potsdam Bridge, its
checkpoint guardhouse guarding unmanned
a country whose national color had been

                      Drab,
and found the Great Frederick's palace:
the cavernous main salon's ceiling and walls
inlaid with sea shells in numbers
rivaling the infinite,

              huge swirls
of pearly conchs, Persian labyrinths knit
of a thousand pink cockles, edged
with lavender winkles.

              For wainscot,
a band of geodes (grapefruit-sized and split
to show the amethyst sea-urchin cores)
and giant quartz crystals like milky shafts
of sunlight in sea water.

              One waltzing brush
would leave the evening gown in tatters.
This I imagined

                        my lustrous and opaline
(if fretful and sedulous) interior life—
brunching on caviar as the Red Army crosses
the lawn, la la—
                        for nothing eggs
the mind to sleights and high-wire antics
like ceaseless painting.
                                I was in trouble, I knew,
when first I savored the whiff of a freshly
opened gallon: that new-car-smell laced
with the Jersey Turnpike
                                and brain damage.
It's not for nothing that painters
drink.
                Far below, soaked t-shirt pressed
to the baking sandpaper of asphalt shingles, lies
my body, but I'm
                        up here,
floating among the feathery leaf tips,
a giddy bouquet of champagne bubbles,
where a sea breeze borne from a hundred miles
brushes the tree tops with
                        Golden Sunshine, and,
hovering here beside me, a hummingbird
decked out in Chromium Madder-Orange ascot
and plush Tawny Sienna waistcoat.
                                I have
counterbalanced the can in the left hand
with the extended right leg
                        at the top
of the extension ladder and mouthed
the instant convert's last-ditch prayer
that the tremor—whether in leg,
                                ladder footing,
or the earth itself—would not
                                come again.
I have earned the wages of the sins of commission
in the unwiped
                        drip, in the freckling

fantail splatter on glass, and suffered, too,
the sins of omission
in the discrete recesses left unpainted
(the soffit's armpit, the stairway's crotch)
                                                not to mention
the neglected brush, its bristles now set
in a permanent rictus.
                        I have bowed, at last,
to the steady practice and the modest reward
of the sure hand and the brush's mastery
and ridden the rolling paint bead's surge
down the line between putty and glass
and known
                the wave's curl—inevitable!—
the surfer riding its crest beachward,
the two
        one.
I have come in the end to a kind of surrender,
the sheer repetition like the mother's heartbeat
heard from within, so that even in sleep
I keep on painting, my dream-arm flapping
like the one
                good wing, me sentenced to wander
the countless
                other rooms at *Sans Souci*—
long stripped by museums or The People's Army,
where gray shadows peel from the ghosts
of paintings, and ceilings recede in cobweb clouds
of bygone, imperial mutterings—
desperately in search of a little
                        color.

BUYING LIPSTICK FOR MY WIFE

The woman in a lab coat with fiercely plucked eyebrows
smiles from behind *Clinique's* resplendent altar:
   glass, chrome, flowers in an onrushing cavalcade.

"I'm married just a year myself," she confesses,
turning and turning the ring on her slim, pale finger,
   but our fifteen has equipped me no better to choose

from this maddening stockpile of siloed missiles,
more shades from brown to blue than Picasso knew,
   row upon row arranged to climb the scale of passion

or indecision, this proliferation the stalemate
to any cold war's meltdown. "Nice ring," she says,
   unscrewing another incendiary hue,

drawing a line on the thickly veined back
of my hand. "My husband thought we'd start
   with these simple bands," but I hear, "triple banns,"

splitting the etymological difference
between "bend" and "bond," bound hand
   to hand, as she draws a fourth line, *Lush Life*

clashing or merging—who could tell?—with *Disco
Inferno.* I'm starting to understand, starting to look
   for shades between shades, a hue too slick

for even the French aficionados of fashion,
the one named *Devil's Tongue* or *Prick de Chein*,
   sliding forth, the fifth line needed to cross.

CAPTAIN SEAWEED, AKA CHECKERS THE CLOWN

*Turn Your Frown Upside Down, For Your Next Party Call Checkers
the Clown Picnics Birthday Parties Corporate Events 321-8079*

—Sign painted on his car door

How many decades can a man sham wonder?—
his belly now thick as a bole on an oak tree,
his labored, smoker's breathing as he exhorts
the children toward another peak of squeals
or, from the older kids, incredulous jeers:
"I saw that, I know how you did that!"

Is there anywhere enough milk of human kindness
to wash down a steady diet of pre-pubescent heckling
and not lie down nights with thoughts of murder?
Though perhaps even worse is the kid like me
who could not enjoy a birthday party clown,
dreading his failure, biting a knuckle each time

the gimcrack gizmo faltered, the covering smile
brightened, the patent saccharine bathed all wounds.
Every clown I meet I want to punch in the face.
And that's how I feel today, my son's birthday,
leaning against the chimney in the converted garage
with the slouching nine-year-old neophyte skeptics

as Captain Seaweed, a bead of sweat rolling now
down from the brim of his skipper's cap, tugs
the red, white, and blue hankies from his fist—
an American flag!—pure propaganda schlock,
though now even the back-row jaws hang slack.
As the *Jiffy* and *Smuckers* jars change places,

the linked rings that a stalwart volunteer couldn't part
juggle freely, the faces in the front row undergo
a change, begin to sharpen, then glow, then open,
until sitting there on their heels with heads tilted back
they want nothing this moment will not give them.
How did he do that, do it again, do it again.

THE SEEDS OF SORROW

> *You have come by way of sorrow*
> *You have come by way of tears*
> *But you'll reach your destiny*
> *Meant to find you all these years*

> —Julie Miller

Why always at the edge of happiness laps this boundless ocean
    of sorrow? I could be
Playing with my children in one of those moments when they laugh
    and nudge one another,
Having just then forgotten the half-share of parental love the other
    daily steals, and, especially then,
Glance away and see it standing all around us, indistinguishable from air,
    not a threat but a promise.

I could be riding to work on the Cherry Creek bike path in September,
    mid-morning sun
Rinsing the concrete clean, hammering the surface of the water that rushes
    along beside me to silver,
The shadow bridge through which I sail a delicious chill, and even the bum,
    sleeping it off beneath,
Comfortable in his army surplus bag, his transistor playing canned classical,
    when all at once

A little breath of wind rises toward a sob, which I must swallow or drown in.
    "What Act of Legislature was there
That *thou* shouldest be Happy?" asked Carlyle, a man like me judgmental
    almost to bitterness,
And his too my ploy: to grind the continuous feedstock of sorrow into anger,
    turning it back upon the world,
That black hole of anger, which never even shrugs, only jerks sorrow's lining
    inside out once more.

Here comes my grandfather, who daily harnessed his wagon to the oxen
    of wrath, who whipped them
To fiery nostrils by reading and rereading *Job*, who earned the five heart attacks
    of which he was proud,
Wobbling punch-drunk from the dentist's office, still doped after a root-canal,
    his fists raised above his head
And crying, "They can't kill me, by God, hard as they try!" And didn't God
    suckle Job on rancor

So he'd break his teeth on the bread of sorrow with blessings, didn't God
      raise his fists in exaltation?
"What if thou wert born and predestined Not to be Happy, but to be Unhappy?"
      Maybe then
We rise up and dance, knowing at last as we had refused till then to know
      that naming it—
Whether in rage, resignation, or praise—alters the condition by an amount
      that would not tip an atomic scale.

Maybe then we lay down our work, that gospel Carlyle preached and our fathers
      served, burning the midnight oil
Of anger to fuel the bigger car to fume away faster, while behind us
      the greenhouse waters of sorrow
Only steal more surely up the shores of our holiday get-aways. Maybe then
      we rise up from our desks,
Raise our fists above our head, and turn, very slowly, our feet tamp-tamping in
      the seeds of sorrow.

SCALPINGS

I.

Come home from his first year of college,
he the first in the family to get on past
high school, to make it out of Baton Rouge
on a football scholarship up north

to Georgia Tech, my grandfather, Papa,
a flaxen beard ghosting his chin,
flopped down on the sway-backed sofa
of childhood for a nap. Waked with a start,

there was his old man astraddle his chest
with a straight-razor raised above his neck.
O, Abraham! His old man, a Louisiana sheriff,
with half a smile on his face, said not a word,

just dry-scraped one half of that new beard away,
dismounted, shifted the smile to the other side,
said not a word, and left him there, a badly
shorn lamb, born again into manhood.

II.

Once, in the early 60s, cloistered
for that moment in a gas-station toilet
with a young man, a boy really, he drew
his pocket knife and, as I imagine it,

while the mannish-boy stood at the urinal
(tall porcelain, gorged with a mini-colander)
took hold of the other's rubber-banded ponytail
and cut it off. Papa told this to me

the summer before I was to leave for college,
my hair already inching toward my collar.
Planning a Louisiana road-trip that summer,
I asked how to find our kin. He forbade me.

There are two signs of a lazy man, he said,
a pool cue in hand, and a pocket knife dull.
Comanche, Sioux—"Injuns," he'd call them—
knew a thing or two about disempowerment.

III.

Earlier, a boy who slipped from shadow to shadow,
who trained his feet to walk straight-forwardly,
who eschewed the cap pistol for the makeshift bow,
I lived in covenant with the light-whispering trees.

Forest and night were sanctuaries of ambush.
Somewhere, in the background, minions of progress
were arriving in choppers. Jehovah gave scalped boys
mouthing Jesus the go-ahead for genocide.

Lord knows, I too confused freedom with license,
choosing to drop out, growing a beard and hair
exactly like those Sunday-school posters of Jesus.
If I come in peace, I always come stealthily,

a stag-handled knife weighing my pocket,
and looking, always, over my shoulder for Jehovah.
I am not such a fool to believe I escaped
the lineage of manhood shocked in my genes.

TENNESSEE LATITUDES

I.
Slender index finger grown
from the colonial fist of the Carolinas,
Tennessee pointed the unknown.

Long hunters and Indian killers
transgressed remote royal decree
and the smoky ranges of the Cherokee

to bind natural boundaries—
the Appalachians' winding emerald divide
to the Mississippi's

dog-legs and intestinal loops—
between imperious latitudes,
the globe's imaginary barrel hoops.

II.
In the heat-stymied spectators' gallery
of Dayton's ante-bellum courthouse
God sat. The fans beat wearily

to Bryan's oration on His behalf.
He declined to take the stand, or so
the *Times* reporter quipped, with a laugh.

Leaving in Pyrrhic defeat, Darrow
observed dryly, "'Tis a long state,
and exceedingly narrow."

III.
But the most neighborly of states,
shouldered snug as a jigsaw piece
amidst the abutting eight,

though it offers a view of far fewer—
despite *Rock City's* barn-roof signs—
now that the skies could be bluer.

Imagine the billboards and firework stands
gone, the freeway unzipped, the smog
vacuumed. There they stand,

peering westward from the gap they rename
"Newfound," the ridges lapping away
to the horizon's unskimmed cream.

Armed with anvils and needles, lenses
and ink, flintlocks and fiddles, maps
trailing into uncharted whiteness

and ribbon-marked beatitudes,
the unknown approaches, hell-bent
on taking wider latitude.

"BLOW, WIND! COME WRACK!"

—for S. T. F., Sr.

To take a concrete example, a train
Nuzzles through dense forest, dusk,
Louisiana, August, 1910.

A sodden current of air rushes in
The window you've slid down to listen
To crickets and peepers shaking the air

Like sleigh bells. The locomotive
Passes from under the mantle of live oaks
Onto a plain of ready ground,

Gray-brown dirt in vanishing furrows,
And out beneath the flatiron sky,
Poised like a vase on a spinning kick-wheel,

A tiny black funnel the size of God.
The train urges its strict line forward.
You sit alone by the window and watch it

Wobbling on a fierce axis, clearing a path
Toward a miniature farmhouse, silo, and barn.
Are those people scurrying there, is that

Your grandfather, a boy, crouching
With his sisters and a chicken in the root-cellar,
Or is it mine? Always it was possible

One of us would not be born,
And what else is it then that excites,
That makes beauty real and really

Insubstantial, seizing moments
As if they were coat hooks, shingles
And gutters, faucets and shutters,

Built into houses and released by the wind,
If not a love of what might happen
Spun into love of what might not?

EXPLAINING TO MY MOTHER WHY THE NEXT WAR
WILL BE NECESSARY

I think of you when the newsreel men with their dramatic
        black-and-white voices told of the Korean Communists,
How they refused our bounty of life in the suburbs, liberty to shop,
        and the pursuit of strictly individual happiness,
Preferring their own mean lot of self-determination. How could you,
        a new bride and pregnant with me, caught up
In the terrible mystery of building a life in the thriving America of the 50s,
        foresee the chain of board-game wars to come?

Even given that vision, how could you deny the Depression dream
        of prosperity bequeathed by your parents
Like a set of hand-tinted daguerreotypes, the memories of real heroes
        marching triumphantly home
From a real war? It may become impossible after so many deaths,
        their cumulative justifications and erasure
Into myth, to see that the "us" in U.S. has become our interest in saving
        "them" from themselves with bombs.

It may be too much for anyone to hold at once the double meanings,
        like those magic plastic cards in *Cracker Jack* boxes:
Held one way, it's the beaming face of Reagan or Bush, the other
        and it's Marcos, the Shah of Iran, or Pinochet;
This way, the nation's monumental white lingam, that way, the spread legs
        of a black granite chevron,
Fifty eight thousand one hundred and thirty two names. It may be
        that history's too close to home to see.

Do you remember the story of the travelers floating at night
        down the wild Tennessee
In the days before the TVA tamed it with locks and dams? How they
        passed on the distant bank a fire,
And saw small figures reveling there, and the fiddle carried a tune
        across the water, "Arkansas Traveler" or "Old Joe Clark,"
How they passed a second fire and marveled the same tune was played
        there also, but on the third pass

Stood silent above their sleeping children and knew they were caught
    in a "suck" sweeping them from bank to bank
In an arc too big to feel. Once again I hear a voice preaching defense
    is priority one, the flags are gaily popping,
The jets roar overhead, our hands rise toward our hearts, for peace
    is surely won by arms proliferating
And a gun in every home. When GI Joe and Jedi knights hook up
    with Sergeant York, and Alan Ladd and Audi Murphy

Join Schwarzenegger and Stallone, then Pokémon will fall right in and all
    will march as one, and kids will go to grammar school
With daddy's *Smith & Wesson*, and vote, when they grow up, to fight
    and teach those bullies a lesson.
I hear a voice crackling from behind a giant-sized mask, "Ignore, ignore,
    ignore, that little man in the booth."
I wake in the night and feel black water sliding away beneath. The band's
    struck up, and it's the same tune that we've heard before.

SOLILOQUY FROM THE *DIALECTIC OF ENLIGHTENMENT*

Knowledge, which is power, knows no limits,
and technology is the essence of this knowledge;
thus, enlightenment is totalitarian, sweet prince,
and bourgeois society is ruled by equivalence.
All gods and qualities must be destroyed,
and the world made subject to man: myth
becomes enlightenment and nature mere objectivity.

The identity of everything with everything is bought
at the cost that nothing can at the same time be
identical to itself. It amputates the incommensurable.
Ouch. The cry of terror called forth by the unfamiliar
becomes its name, by which one can see the essence of gods
is not exhausted by individuality. Regrettably, both reason
and religion outlaw the principle of magic,

but language thereby becomes more than a mere
system of signs, and mathematical procedure
becomes a kind of ritual of thought. Go figure.
There is no being in the world that knowledge
cannot penetrate, but what can be penetrated
by knowledge is not being. Do be a do bee.
The equation of mind and world is finally resolved,

but only in the sense that both sides cancel out.
Enlightenment thereby regresses to the myth-
ology it has never been able to escape:
animism had endowed things with souls;
industrialism makes souls into things. Cha-ching.
Individuals define themselves now only as
statistical elements, successes and failures,

and the control of external and internal nature
has been made the absolute purpose of life, for which
the epic already contains the correct theory:
the curse of irresistible progress is irresistible
regression. The over-ripeness of society lives
on the immaturity of the ruled. We're fucked,
though real history (still) is woven from real suffering.

BREANNA'S GRANDMOTHER
(Sunridge Apartments, Sacramento, CA)

Saturday mornings that summer, the roof tar
Already bubbling six inches above our ceiling,
The couple beneath us would begin to accelerate
Toward exploding crockery, sunglasses for the woman.

I'd ease to the window, part the blinds with a finger,
As if expecting gunmen, and scan the vacant
Parking slots, each anointed with a black rose
Of many overlaid oil stains. Sometimes,

Breanna's grandmother would part her blinds
On the other side of the sun-heaved drive,
And for that moment we'd look directly
At one another. But mostly

We looked the other way and avoided asking.
She never asked how a family could afford
To drive a continent, then camp in unfurnished rooms.
I never asked the name she declined to give

When I gave mine, so I too called her "Breanna's
Mother," even though in walking her hips seemed driven
By disjointed flywheels, and the lines in her face
Told decades more than a mother's cares. Mostly,

We sat by the pool as the traffic whiffled past
On San Juan Avenue and watched our girls,
Barefoot on scalding pavement, dance
From shadow to shadow, then practice

Frog jumps into the aqua-blue box of water.
After weeks of sitting nearly together,
Her in her shift and stockings rolled
To smooth tourniquets beneath her knee wattles,

Me having leaped from a *Land's End* catalog
But with a plastic cup of *San Miguel* tequila,
I ventured to ask. "My son," she said, "he died,
I haven't seen the mother since the day of the birth,

The landlord says if my other son comes round
He'll evict us, can he do that?" The girls,
Sleek and round-bellied in floral suits,
Dog paddled precariously, but undulated like seals

Beneath the surface, gliding through petals of sunlight
As if all one needs is to trust the medium.
But whenever the heads went under she
Would lean forward and cry, "Bree, Bree,"

Never having learned to swim herself.
In her recurring dream, Breanna sinks downward,
Eyes lifted, one arm raised, while she
Kneels by the pool-side and cries the name,

Seized by the choice to join her there
Or go on living each moment longing
Breanna will kick her heels and rise.
By the time we packed the minivan to leave,

I'd turned the girls from tadpoles to frogs,
Kicking in spurts across the surface,
But she left my offer to give her a lesson
Unanswered. After all, what could I,

Who always held a prepaid ticket back
To the suburbs, tell her? What did I know,
What do I know, of the medium in which
She has no choice each day but swim?

BEGGING THE DEAD

The trees are more themselves for being bare;
the sky, too, for being held by the trees,
and bluer for being colder.

You play in a spill of leaves beside the road,
kick loosening sheaves of color
into the air. The breeze

lifts a red leaf, you follow, a car looms
and swings past, your reflection
sliding across its chrome,

sliding a shaft of ice into my heart, my hands
fly up to reach through glass,
span the yard, pull you safe.

And then I see them: your great aunt, unhusbanded
and stripped of child by faceless men
hurtling the freeway drunk;

your aunt, my sister, just old enough to drive
when the phone call came past midnight.
Do recurring loses build

a curse, or work a talisman against them?
The trees are more themselves for being
bare; the sky, too,

for being held by the trees, and bluer for being
colder. *I beg you, do not be jealous*
for his company too soon.

FACING THE ELK

Rex, the cowboy campground host, told us
it was a bear ate the guts out of that elk.
Em and I had hiked up along the creek,
through a meadow where grasshoppers crackled
suddenly into the heat-stilled air,
snapping their cellophane wings like party favors.

The trail dropped down along a cool bend
where the grasses seemed the thick hair of naiads
combed by paralleling currents of wind,
then climbed through stands of aspen and spruce,
opening and flattening briefly before the gorge
narrowed to its boulder-crowded ascent.

It was there I first smelled it and asked Em
to walk behind me, jingling my keys
to warn the living, ward off the dead.
Keys that opened nothing there, a primitive
instrument for playing the jangled chords of fear,
a talisman singing, *door lock cave...*

You know the place, if only in dream:
nostrils flare around a scent, sunlight shudders
down through close branches and dims, legs,
braced for flight, freeze, and—as if slowly—
something explodes out of your blind spot.
Or so it seems for those who only imagine it.

And we do, endlessly, playing and replaying
lapsed responses loosely wired in the brain,
polished now to a voyeuristic luster
by longer lenses and special effects, the hushed
musical accents of scientific wonder.
God save us from a death that is homely,

ordinary, soggy with doubt, or merely lonely.
Better to end like this: legs broken under us,
muzzle twisted to the sky in the grimace
of *Guernica's* horse, ribs harrowing the wind,
empty as a scooped-out melon, embraced
by the avaricious love of maggots. What a lie.

An older version of the "old lie," as Wilfred Owen
called it, but we seem never to be unconvinced
and so must look, look again, fill our nostrils
until they are socks stuffed with rotting mackerel.
Why should I have been surprised, then,
when the next day, planning our hike, Em—

who had shielded her eyes and squeezed my hand,
and complained of an image she could not shake
from her head, and seen in the spokes of shadow
cast by our campfire the forms a bear might take
in stalking—asked to go that way again,
to face, to give the one familiar face, to fear.

HOMOSASSA

—for W.H.T.

Though we're a month before high season,
the *Homosassa Inn* is booked with fishermen.
Down at the docks, the scaling boards

are swaled from scraping, the boxy fuel pumps
stand at ease. Sunset brings the boats in,
coolers packed with lead-eyed rainbows,

the odd striped bass or jack cravalle.
Across the river, the two-story Victorian,
its attendant live oaks, where you and Momsey

came for weeks of fishing when the roads
were sand-ruts all the way from US1.
Today, without you, we head for the maze

of rush flats and tidal alleys, swinging
between palmetto-crowded banks
as if the boat were hung from a string—

while clouds, flushed and wind-raked, look down
on an insect winding a Persian rug.
The outboard's thrumming roar brings us

each moment to the verge of a quietness
it shatters, but fish jump in our wake.
One rolling dorsal unzips the surface,

a gar, the gangster of brackish water.
A Seminole shell mound takes us unaware,
its chalky dome like a ruined cathedral.

We startle an anhinga from its crucifix pose.
Then, the zone of ethereal glades,
sudden white birds like puppets got up

from sticks and ripped sheets, a place
neither fully land's nor water's. The sun
slips up, already hot by seven, too hot,

you reckoned last night from your bedside phone,
for trout to seek refuge from the deeper cold.
So we drift and cast in open water, watch

for flashes of lamé threading the eel-grass,
and just when its billow and whiplash threaten
to lull us into a trance—a strike!

Off shore, the factory trawlers spread
their gill nets, but one boat of anglers
caught the limit yesterday. I asked

at the *Riverside's* dock about Sam Lyle.
He's pushing ninety and "don't get out much."
His grandson, Buckie, is guiding now.

DRUCKER'S MULE BARN

Hell, it didn't even have a phone, what
was I thinking? By the time of that obscene squawk-box
the mule was nearly obsolete, except maybe
in Ecuador. Maybe the phone extincted the mule,
but I'd dial the barn right now if anyone could answer.

There they are, standing in the boxy stalls,
there's Jake, beard-stubble dun, one ear
turreted straight back, chewing in slow motion,
and there's Boxer with a blue hoof cocked
as you walk gingerly behind, and then Manchu—
"yellow-slant-eyed-wicked-bastard,"
Uncle Don hisses at him—almost invisible
in the sun-spatter of hay-light through the slats,
and there at the end, The Reverend, as Rodney
dubbed him, by turns solemn and ecclesiastical
with wrath, shiny black as a cheap Sunday suit.

I don't know how to get back there now,
though curls of dust from our passing still settle
down through the hushed air on the old turnpike.
The poplars, pin oaks, and shagbark hickories
that yellow the roof of the road's tunnel in fall
rustle green still with invisible passings.

But there it is, I swear to God, at the dogleg
where the creek bends behind, up ahead on the left,
that gray hulk of timber and tin with the doors
swung wide, Uncle Don and Rodney out front
in their washed-out *Pointer Brand* overalls,
passing the black twist of *Black Mariah*.
They still know how to talk to a mule
the way a mule needs to be talked to
when it baulks, when it hesitates between
narcolepsy and the urge to crush you utterly,
when it cogitates the somber truths.

I need those somber truths now,
and narry a mule around. Not infrequently
I need the instruction of one who knows
how to grind resentment into patience. I need
to pace myself, I need some mule time,
I need the bitter consolation and the succor
of sweet hay, dusk, fly-buzz, slant sun.

That's why when someone I don't know
and don't want to know rings my phone
I sometimes pick it up and say, "Drucker's
Mule Barn." For all I know a Goddamn interstate's
been laid smack on top of that turnpike,
barn, mules, creek, and trees just
a foiled layer of sediment in a fossil's seam,
and no one there, when the non-existent phone
begins inaudibly to ring and ring and ring,
to answer.

IV. Grace Given Back

Come, lean your light
foot
    on the lily, and rise forever
on the dark unhurried waters of descending.

               —Andrew Hudgins,
                "The Lake Sings to the Sleepless Child"

LOUIE LOUIE

Places are made of names we take for granted,
like "Signal Mountain," named by Confederates
who mirrored flashes of intelligence to the valley,
or "James Boulevard," the road of our Brown House,
a busy street, mother reminded me with a forsythia
switch to the back of my bare legs at six.
"James" for the Bible king, or for father?

But names hold meanings we experience
unknowingly. Sid Henry bit the back
of my bare calf in the basement of the First
Presbyterian Church. I still don't understand
getting bit, or what "Presbyterian" means,
though stern retribution seems part of it.
We spread our blankets on the cool, hard

terrazzo floor for nap-time, though "terrazzo"
would come later. Some kids had pastel pink
or green binkies. My white terrycloth bathmat,
with a few kidney beans of rust stain,
protected me—a Sid-less island smelling of mother.
The fluorescents flickered out. My mouth shaped,
flower essence. The dim, cool basement swayed

as the traffic on James Boulevard passed
in shushing waves…We rose with patterned faces.
I crossed the street, looking both ways,
and walked the sidewalk, stepping over cracks.
Though we did not own a radio, I had heard
"Louie Louie," and Andrew Spitler said
it was about sex. Could "Louie" be a code name

(mirror flashes?) or just the name of a girl? Oh baby,
what's "sex" but a name for something no one
understands? *I gotta go, yeh yeh yeh yeh yeh,* but
I crossed my legs and held it. *I sailed the ship
all alone* (the traffic on James Boulevard shushing),
I wondered when I'm gonna make it home.
"Home" is a name for a place no one understands,

though that would come later. My homework
blew out of my hands, a sheet of paper white
as my bathmat, and I darted out to grab it:
behind me, a squealing noise, an elephant charge.
Let's call it "the past," the name of a place
no one ever reaches, so unknowingly
the meanings and names and places become us.

COOKIN' WITH THE DAVID JONES TRIO

Life is fun when you're good at something good.
—William Matthews

In Saturday's kitchen in jeans,
                    Dad wound-up his wrist,
          looping the fat yolks

into a pinwheel of yellows,
                    concentrating ease
          into speed, and just let

go, let the greased
                    sockets of the wrist spin
          on the elbow's flywheel, let

the eggs, as if by their own
                    momentum, merge into
          a smear of galaxy and rise

with the ring of the whisk to fine-
                    beaded froth. Last night,
          the jazz trio's pianist

urged the first few notes
                    from between his shoulders, listening,
          eyes closed, for them

to alight somewhere far
                    away, then followed or
          was pulled along like a man after

spilled papers, the wind
                    cartwheeling them now in overlapping
          riffs, shavings of sunlight

tumbling across the emerald
                    lawn and down the rumpled
          hillside into the shade-steeped

funk beneath the trees where
                    the bassman joined him,
          approaching thunder felt

in the ground, in the bones, startling
                        a flung fist of starlings
            from beneath the eaves of

the baby grand, a swoop
                        of notes dispersing, satin
            shadows rippling across

hedgerow and rock-wall off
                        the fringe-lipped precipice,
            the drummer's snare and slash

of cymbals, the foot-pedaled
                        drum jumping hearts
            into our throats and out

above the dazzling waves,
                        miraculous suspension, oh,
            take me, let me go

let me hover in the wind's
                        chamber, drift up and
            eddy in a thermal, even

as horizon comes a sweep
                        of thunderhead, hot rain
            strafing the city, its

soot-grimed cars riddled
                        with leopard spots, tenement
            windows rattling prismatic

streaks, a whale's moan
                        of sweet anguish from a thumb
            drawn across the conga's

skin, the arse-end
                        of a handle sliding down
            the cymbal's brass spine,

and ending when the eggs hit
        the skillet, the sizzle buttering
    our appetites for artifice made

natural, grace given back
        by hands that thank. Thank you,
    Dad, Daddy, Daddio.

SPICE

As in the spice of, as in
put some back into your,
as in the plural of
spouse, as in
what you need is
a little, as in hotter.

As in eons of sweetening
the seed for avian
disbursement,
embittering leaves
against bark-boring
insects, as in perpetuity
guaranteed
by seducing the dominant
species with spices.

As in spices for specie,
the spoil and offering
of kings. As in
forty-one days of nights
tracking the star paths
to chart the Moluccas,
bilk the Venetian
land-route monopoly,
barter or kill, pack
barrels and inlaid
teak chests full
of bark, buds, pods, corns, stems,
and connect the celestial
dots homeward.
As in gold.

As in the supermarket aisle's
most suggestive
alphabet, especially
the Cs: caraway,
cardamome, cassia,
modest chervil, immodest
chili, cinnamon's
exotic coziness,

the cloven hooves
of cloves, coriander
and her brother
cilantro, and cumin
that flares the nostrils
like fresh oak sawdust,
but loamier, danker, rank
with complexity, almost
animal.

As in all of the foods—
Indian, Mexican, Thai—
that Emma, age six,
says are "too,"
observing in the shower
peppermint soap
in her crotch feels
"spicy, oh spicy,
oh oh oh,"
as in on the way to
everything nice.

DEAR TOOTH FAIRY,

The close, dark rooms of childhood
reared with acetylene shadows
    when you burst in like a mini-supernova.

I wish just once I had awakened
when your iridescent sea-urchin quills
    brushed my cheek and seen you there,

not as Disney or even I
imagine you, but as you are:
    a compact, inexpressible miracle

of natural reward, rare now
as hen's teeth. What do you do
    with all of those little milky corns—

sow them anew in bubble-gum mouths,
grind them to sweet-dream powder,
    set them as fairy's washstands?

Some turn up decades later
in the backs of jewelry drawers, sharp
    as regret. Some return to the earth.

And do you harvest the unbudded rows
of stillborns, or enter the dark-slit mouths
    to claim what breath has left behind?

Like my daughter, who this year begins
to know the questions to leave unasked,
    I don't want to know everything yet,

however long in the tooth I grow.
It's her example I follow, writing you,
    she who each time now enfolds

her tooth with block-lettered questions:
"What's your name?" or "How old are you?"
    Forgive me for reading your mail,

presuming to answer in your hand:
"It cannot be said in human tongue," or
  "I am as old as time is young." Like her,

I leave this under my pillow wishing
if only one last time you'll come
  (and not too soon some things come true).

THE ANTHROPOLOGY OF LITTLE LEAGUE BASEBALL

The styles of neophyte umpires alone merit
A monograph from a small distinguished press,

This one's elaborate Kung-Fu-inflected step
Twist, plunge, and recoil—"YROUT!"—

With the sound of wind punched out of bagpipes, or
The stately, vulnerable posturing of last week's ump

As he dropped from the waist to sweep home plate
With the same six precisely parallel brusque strokes.

A field-seasoned prof with a team of grad interns
Might well forego that sub-Saharan nomadic tribe

To lurk these stands, scribbling notes, convening
Each evening over the beverage favored by locals

To discuss the genres and signatures of spitting
Among rural American ten-year-old boys—girls

Now too—back pockets bulging with pouches
Of shredded pink bubblegum "chew." They might devise

A special calligraphy to note the choreography
Of sliding, the balletics of snag and tag, and especially

The beautiful contortions of pitchers' windups: the little
Prayer over the ball, the shock-corded limbs

Arcanely folded, unsprung with unlikely grace.
One intern adept in confessional interviews,

Practiced in native dialect and vernacular, will sit
Among the parents, the grandparents, the step-parents,

And ask, "So, which one's yours?", which, he knows,
Will unfold stories of fathers, the early victories

That ease the world's disregard, the healing rites
Of eternal seasonal return, the allegiance we pledge

To sportsmanship, as long as we're winning, team spirit
Plus the free-agent slinging greased-lightning sliders.

One whimsical ethnographer may linger
In stands emptied of all but wrappers and cups

And witness the invisible cloud that hovers
Above the arc-lit diamond, the collective

Night-cherished fantasy of playing in the Majors,
Which only a few seasons can sustain.

ELEMENTAL

—*for Gay Wilentz, 1950-2006*

The Paradise restaurant's palm-thatch cabana
overlooks the island's graveyard. The salt's
in a screw-top jar, the sugar in a capped bottle.

Last night's wanly blinking Christmas lights
drape the dry fountain, the concrete flamingo,
its re-bar legs dwindling with rust. Concrete's

the new answer here: wood huts on stilts
give way to block haciendas. Even the dead
have concrete crosses and pillbox sarcophagi.

Beyond the graveyard, a "w" of palm trees,
a wooden sloop at anchor, the far line of breakers.
Hurricane Mitch broke some markers, floated

some boxes—though no one swam away,
it looks like they had one hell of a party.
The salt in its jar, the sugar in its bottle.

The palms frame the boat, the boat gleams
thick brushstrokes of turquoise and tamarind,
the reef smokes, an acetylene weld the sun

just laid down. A quiet waiter serves us
fried eggs tinctured with blood, burnt coffee.
Pale children run to the palms to join

a black boy and a brown boy, take turns
kicking off from the palms on a rope swing.
Salt air, it changes the chemistry of everything.

A battalion of the smallest ants imaginable
braids a loose helix up the white stucco wall—
sign of the invisible suture joining everything.

A child kicks off, disappears in a wink of sun.
One might do worse than become elemental,
love moisture like salt, love ants like sugar.

KAKADU CAVE PAINTINGS

Limned in ochre
and zinc-white on sandstone,
the Big Ancestor's
head's a fish.

Legs like jack-knifed
Eiffel Towers
assume the Sumo's
ready squat, allow

the turtle's sinewed
neck and hungry maw
of his dick to dangle
inquisitively.

His skeletal bride,
antennae piqued,
skips the digital rope
of her many toe bones,

while from out the
cable-swung dredger jaws
of her vulva swim
x-rays of flounders,

whose ribs become
radiant spokes crowning
the host of tribal mothers.
Maybe halos.

LAPPING, SWIMMINGLY

—for Mary Ann Samyn

Flickering there an impressionistic
childbirth documentary, but from
inside
      the emerging perspective—all dewdrop
on eyelash, all spangled and rainbowy—

but then I'm working
           so hard so hard
to get out, or there, to the other end of
where?—
      I don't know, that's what could be
terrifying, though instead it's merely

the process: the inescapable body
escaping immersion in its own
               internal element,
so doubly
      suspended, sinking while lifted,
but barely, and bare, stripped down and

self-propelled by a
          rhythm—breathe
stroke stroke stroke
          breathe—and so on,
though even if drowning (perhaps even
heightened by) one still might admire

the hypnotic, spider-webby expansion,
the prismatic
        wobble, the honey-comb
fractal, a living
        model of chaos (is that
singular?), which requires order (a pattern

plus repetition, riffing, arithmetic,
all only seemingly
        random) in order
to exist. Such a thin membrane
between the self and
        dissolution.

WHAT THE RAIN SAID THIS MORNING

Go back to sleep. Don't go
back to sleep. Listen.

Your body could be this
patternless patter, this

patterless pattern. Yes,
that's it. No,

don't be sad, or be sad
like this. Give in

not up. Listen.
Be a leaf, wait, expect nothing.

Be green, drink
this sound. Fall. There is nothing

that will not welcome you.
There is a rhythm inside you

other than the one set
to go off. Don't

get up. Get in
to your burrow. Smell your fur, drying,

and the familiar dirt. Listen.
The earth is a drum. Your organs

are drums like burrows, every cell
a burrow like a drum. In each

you are the animal. On each
you rain.

JUDY AS PIÑATA

Blindfolded, a boy with a stick,
  encircled by friends, swings
 wide parabolas, always

just missing
  the pink crepe-paper-tufted she-ass
 that floats above his head

unwaveringly,
  until, as if knowing then
 the center of all

empty arcs, he
  strikes home: a rain
 of cheers and treasures and hands.

I stand with a baby in my arms,
  our family gathered round, those
 living and, behind them,

all our dead, and you
  are floating, floating above us,
 rosy, empty, and whole.

A NOTE ON THE AUTHOR

Jeffrey Franklin grew up in Chattanooga, Tennessee. He holds degrees from the Baylor School, the University of North Carolina, the Georgia Institute of Technology, and the University of Florida. His poems have appeared in such journals as *The Hudson Review, Measure, New England Review,* and *Shenandoah,* as well as in *Best American Poetry (2002).* His book, *Serious Play: The Cultural Form of the Nineteenth-Century Realist Novel,* appeared in 1999, and a second scholarly book, *Victorian Buddhism: Literary and Cultural Constructions of Buddhism in Nineteenth-Century Britain,* is forthcoming.. He teaches Victorian literature and creative writing at the University of Colorado at Denver, where he lives with his wife, Judy Lucas, and their children, Tyler and Emma.

Printed in the United States
60903LVS00003B/34-102